Original title:
Branching Out

Copyright © 2025 Creative Arts Management OÜ
All rights reserved.

Author: Beckett Sinclair
ISBN HARDBACK: 978-1-80567-232-6
ISBN PAPERBACK: 978-1-80567-531-0

New Leaves in the Wind

A leaf danced high, in a breezy style,
Waving to a squirrel, who paused for a while.
They laughed at the clouds, so fluffy and white,
While planning a picnic, in the warm sunlight.

Grass tickled toes, as they joined the fun,
In a game of tag, they both tried to run.
With a butterfly referee, wings all aglow,
They stumbled and tumbled, in the breezy flow.

The Pulse of Discovery

One day a twig, found a new hat,
Made of bright berries, fit for a cat!
It strutted around, feeling so grand,
Till a robin declared, "You're in wonderland!"

They gathered up treasures, shiny and bright,
A bottle cap crown, they wore with delight.
With giggles and glitter, oh what a sight,
Finding joy in the silly, from morning to night.

Visions of What Could Be

A squirrel sat dreaming, of nuts made of cheese,
With a side of potatoes, to savor with ease.
His pals rolled their eyes, but joined in the schemes,
Inventing new recipes, fueled by their dreams.

With leaves as their plates, they feasted and played,
As acorns and twigs formed their grand charade.
In a world full of giggles, they made their decree,
The best meals are made with laughter, you see!

Paintings on a Canvas of Time

I spilled my coffee on the floor,
It looked like art. I need some more.
My mop became a brush today,
Creating chaos in a funny way.

The clock ticks loud, it mocks my pace,
As I dance in socks, a silly grace.
Each moment colored bright with glee,
In this gallery, just me and me.

The Wind's Guiding Hand

The wind blew in, my hat took flight,
It danced around, what a silly sight!
Chasing it down felt like a race,
I laughed so hard, fell flat on my face.

Kites overhead with faces so grand,
They made me feel like a part of the band.
I joined the show, twirled and spun,
Under the sky, laughing in the sun.

Whims of the Wanderer

With a map upside down, I roam,
Finding the path to anyone's home.
Each step I take, a giggle confides,
My compass spins, but fun never hides.

The trees are tall, they wave and cheer,
I give a dance, and they all jeer.
An explorer lost, but who cares?
Adventures wait in the laughter it shares.

Sunrises of Change

With breakfast burnt, I made a face,
A toast catastrophe, whose fault? The space!
I declared a feast of charred delight,
And squirrels joined for a morning bite.

As shadows stretch in the dawn's warm light,
I trip on a rug, what a silly sight.
Every new day brings laughter anew,
In this wacky world, it's just me and you.

The Rise of New Horizons

A squirrel with a hat, so profound,
Chasing dreams on the ground.
He looks for acorns, shiny and round,
While plotting his rise, so unwound.

With a wink and a leap, he takes flight,
Bouncing on clouds, oh what a sight!
He yells to the sun, 'Let's party tonight!'
In this silly world, it feels just right.

Cultivating the Unknown

A garden of socks, growing with flair,
With shoes as their petals, like they don't care.
They wiggle and dance in the warm summer air,
When worn by a cat, it's a sight rare!

Potatoes in sunglasses lounge by the fence,
Debating if carrots make more sense.
With laughter and cheer, they break the suspense,
For this garden is wild, without pretense!

Threads of Destiny

A spider named Larry spins tales so grand,
Of gnomes and their quests in a faraway land.
His webs catch the stories, all delicately planned,
While nibbling on pizza, so carefully manned.

In a world made of yarn, where chaos can dance,
Frogs play the fiddles, while lizards prance.
They thread through the night in a glorious trance,
Oh, the joy of it all — just give it a chance!

Reflections on a New Dawn

A rooster named Rufus is starting his day,
In shades and a bowtie, he's ready to play.
He crows out a tune in a jazzy way,
Making all of the hens shout, 'Hip-hip-hooray!'

The sun peeks up, with a wink and a grin,
As cats draw their curtains and prepare to go in.
They tiptoe through dreams, avoiding all sin,
In a world full of giggles, let the fun begin!

The Call of the Unseen

There's a whisper from the trees,
As squirrels throw acorns with glee.
They giggle, toss, and take a chance,
Inviting us to join the dance.

Peeking behind a leafy door,
Adventure calls, who could want more?
A raccoon winks as he scurries wide,
With snacks in hand, come take a ride!

Seeds of Exploration

A sunflower dreams of far-off lands,
While ladybugs form rock band bands.
With beetle drums and a snail on keys,
They jam beneath the swaying trees.

Each seed chuckles as it's tossed,
Into the breeze, oh, what a cost!
With every skip, a new surprise,
A garden party in the skies!

Palettes of the Unknown

In colors bold, the world unfolds,
With crayon rain that brightly holds.
A palette tossed in a playful way,
Painting secrets for kids to play.

Greenish blue and orange twist,
In muddy puddles, you can't resist.
Just jump right in, splashes galore,
Who knew that mud could be such a chore?

Uncharted Terrains

A map made of ice cream and dreams,
With chocolate rivers and marshmallow beams.
Let's venture forth, no need for shoes,
Barefoot explorers, what could we lose?

On a cookie crumb mountain we climb,
Singing our favorite rhymes in time.
With gummy bears as our trusty crew,
Every step's a flavor, bright and new!

The Unseen Pathways

In the yard, I found a way,
A squirrel's path led me astray.
Through bushes thick and weeds so wide,
I danced and twirled, a joyride sly.

The fence looked tall, but I took a leap,
Into the world where secrets creep.
A garden gnome waved 'Hello!'
I tripped on roots, what a show!

My dog thought this was a grand parade,
Chasing shadows, he misplayed.
I lost my hat, but found a shoe,
Along the way, the world felt new.

Up in a tree, I made a friend,
A bird who talked, 'This isn't the end!'
So here I stand, quite out of breath,
Yet loving life, I mock the death.

Expanding Horizons

In a box, I put my dreams,
Thought I'd send them down the streams.
But my cat sat on the lid,
Now my plans are on the grid!

I tried to fly, with wings on back,
But fell straight down, what a whack!
Neighbors laughed, their glee was bright,
As I lay sprawled, a comical sight.

So off I went, with maps in hand,
Exploring realms so unplanned.
I ended up in a pizza place,
Eating slices; I found my grace.

The skies expanded, bright and new,
As my clumsy steps led me to stew.
With laughter ringing, I'll share my tale,
Of silly trips that made me pale.

Sprouts of New Beginnings

In my garden, ninja gnomes grow,
With tiny swords, ready to show.
They teach the plants to do karate,
Making every leaf a little party.

Each morning brings a sprout so bright,
Dancing daisies, what a sight!
But wait, is that a rogue broccoli?
Plotting mischief, I cannot see!

I've watered joy in every pot,
Hoping for magic, a grand jackpot.
Instead, I got weeds with double-talk,
Planting jokes on my afternoon walk.

With laughter sprouting in sunlight's glow,
New beginnings keep stealing the show.
I'll garden on, with quirk and cheer,
As every seed whispers, "Have no fear!"

Paths Unfolding

I stumbled on a folding chair,
Thought I found a path somewhere.
But it folded up, my balance gone,
The ground was sweet, but I rolled on.

Through puddles deep, trials ensue,
Finding treasure just for me and you.
A turtle winked, I tried to race,
But he just laughed and took my place.

The sidewalks called, paved and bold,
With stories waiting to be told.
I met a kid who flew a kite,
We chased the clouds, what a delight!

With every twist and turn I took,
I scribbled thoughts in my old book.
Paths unfold like pages new,
In a book of laughs, my life's debut.

Skyward Aspirations

A squirrel climbs a snack-filled tree,
Dreams of acorns, wild and free.
Up he goes, with leaps and bounds,
Tripping over branches, yet safe and sound.

His friends below start rolling eyes,
As he brags about reaching the skies.
"Look at me! I'm the acorn king!"
While their laughter makes the forest sing.

But winds blow strong, a breeze takes hold,
He wiggles and giggles, oh so bold.
Swinging wildly like a feathered hat,
He lands in a pile, and that's where it's at!

With new plans laid for the next great climb,
He'll conquer the woods, but just not at this time.

Echoes of Evolution

A turtle raced with a hare so fleet,
Both shouting 'First!' to the same old beat.
Each thought they'd win in their own fine style,
But nature laughed—oh, let's stay awhile!

The hare took a nap, snoozing quite proud,
While the turtle hummed, gathering a crowd.
"Slow and steady wins the day," they cheered,
But the turtle's dance was what they truly feared.

He moonwalked past, with moves so slick,
The crowd erupted—was that a magic trick?
Every slow beat became a grand show,
As the hare woke up, saying, "Oh no!"

In a twist of fate, both learned to share,
A lesson in laughs, with joy in the air.

Foraging for Freedom

A raccoon in search of a midnight feast,
Fumbles around, to say the least.
He trips on a can, then does a spin,
"Who knew this trash bin could be my win?"

With a bag on his head, he starts to prance,
Shuffling around like he's in a dance.
His pal the skunk, with a knowing grin,
Says, "Dude, you've really lost your skin!"

They ally together, in the moon's soft glow,
Sharing their snacks and avoiding woe.
With giggles and grins, their laughter so loud,
These foraging pals, they're quite the crowd!

As dawn approaches, they make a pact,
To keep on exploring, and never look back.

Cultivating Chances

A gardener dreams of plants so grand,
Potted hopes, the soil at hand.
He waters and waits, with a curious glance,
Hoping to grow a veggie dance.

But seeds start sprouting with zany flair,
A chorus of carrots fills up the air.
"Are we diving deep?" yells a cheeky pea,
While the lettuce laughs, "Just let it be!"

As radishes wiggle, with tops held high,
The gardener chuckles, "Oh my, oh my!"
What was meant to be dinner, is now a show,
Dancing veggies in a colorful row.

With humor in tendrils, he prances about,
For gardening's magic is without a doubt.

Shifting Landscapes

In a world where trees wear hats,
And squirrels break dance like acrobats,
The flowers gossip in the breeze,
While bees form bands with buzzing keys.

Rocks roll down like they've got a plan,
And rivers leap as if they can,
The hills wear socks, oh what a sight,
As clouds play tag from morn till night.

Mountains laugh at their own height,
While valleys cheer, it's pure delight,
The sun wears glasses, gets in the mix,
Painting rainbows with his light tricks.

What a riot this land of play,
Where nature fools us every day,
The grass does cartwheels, oh so spry,
Who knew? The earth loves to fly!

The Pursuit of the Possible

A cat on a skateboard zooms past me,
Chasing its dreams, oh can't you see?
Pigs fly by with joyful little squeals,
In a world where laughter truly heals.

Wombats in suits, signing a deal,
While turtles negotiate with a wheel,
Chasing horizons, they start to race,
A dizzying world, a wild chase.

Rainbows wear sneakers, ready to run,
Their colors twirling, oh what fun!
Each step a giggle, each leap a yelp,
In this circus of joy, it's hard to help.

With creatures that dream and dance with flair,
Every odd couple make a rare pair,
In the pursuit of what we seek,
Life's just a joke, let's all have a peak!

The Art of Letting Go

A balloon floats high, waves goodbye,
It giggles gently, oh so sly,
A leaf joins in on the dance,
Frolicking away without a chance.

Old shoes left behind on the road,
They tell stories of the heavy load,
While ants march on, with treasures grand,
Letting go of grains, a tasty strand.

The wind whispers secrets, soft and low,
Encouraging us to let emotions flow,
Like a tumbleweed lost in a game,
Where freedom's the prize, and joy's the aim.

So laugh with each tear, embrace the new,
Let the past take a long overdue cue,
In this art of carefree zest,
We find ourselves and feel our best!

Curves and Corners of Tomorrow

Riding a wave on a buttered toast,
A jam jar surfing, you can bet the most,
The future's bright with its silly tune,
Dancing through life like a jazzy cartoon.

Hedgehogs listen to the news each day,
While platypuses sing and sway,
The corners of time make silly jokes,
Where each tick-tock pops out a smoke.

Marshmallows tumble down the slide,
Bouncing with glee, they never hide,
As cookies roll across the green,
In this zany future, nothing's routine.

So grab a hat and join the fun,
With curves of laughter, we've just begun,
In the corners of tomorrow's glow,
We'll find our joy, let's steal the show!

The Fray of Foliage

In the garden, leaves argue,
Who's the best shade of green?
One tries to be a show-off,
While the other remains serene.

Grapevines gossip over wine,
Complaining how trees block the sun,
Laughter rustles through the air,
As flowers burst out, having fun.

A dandelion says with pride,
"Look how far I blow my seeds!"
But the bamboo just sways by,
"I'll grow taller than your deeds!"

Each turn in this leaf-filled fray,
Nature's humor is a must.
We giggle at the folly here,
In the playful dance of dust.

Fractals of Life

Life's a puzzle, piece by piece,
Like fractals, quirky and wild.
One swirl leads to another,
Each twist makes us like a child.

A tree with arms in every style,
Waves at clouds, all fluffy and fat.
"Come join me for a little dance!"
Says the branch to a passing bat.

Bushes nod with awkward grace,
Moss groans, just trying to chill.
Peeking through a honeysuckle,
"Life's a ride—hold on for the thrill!"

Snapdragons crack little jokes,
As petals flutter in glee.
A riot of pattern unfolds,
In this whimsical tapestry.

Spreading Horizons

Clouds surf across a blue sky,
While sunbeams race to join the fun.
A butterfly joins the party,
Dancing under the radiant sun.

A squirrel with style hops along,
Making sure to strut and prance.
It tosses seeds to the wind,
"I'm the king of the forest dance!"

Fields of daisies wink and sway,
Singing tunes of carefree play.
Each bloom bursts with laughter bright,
As day turns into cheeky night.

"Let's grow wild!" the flowers shout,
"Let's explore what's over there!"
In this world of giggles and cheer,
Every moment's a breath of fresh air!

Winding Journeys

A snail decided to race fast,
With dreams of winning the big prize.
In the garden, all eyes were on,
His trail of glittering, slimy lies.

The beetle cheered, "You're the best!"
But tripped on a leaf of green.
Off he tumbled, round and round,
And landed on a potted bean.

A worm poked out to take a peek,
Said, "You think you've got it made?"
But missed the punchline on the joke,
And fell back in, quite dismayed.

With giggles carried on the breeze,
Nature's pranks unfold with flair.
These winding paths full of wit,
Lead us all to the laughter we share.

Fractals of Destiny

In life's great puzzle, pieces collide,
My pizza's toppings, they run and they hide.
Try anchovies here, and pineapple there,
A culinary quest, my taste buds declare!

With every new slice, a rule is defied,
My friends watch in awe, some laughter, some cried.
But at each new bite, adventures begin,
This fractal of flavor, where chaos can win!

Echoes of Exploration

I ventured outside with a map upside down,
Questing for treasures in my sleepy town.
Found a duck pond that quacked like a king,
And a squirrel that danced — oh, what a wild fling!

With each twist and turn, confusion took hold,
I might be lost, but I'm bold, never cold.
Echoes of giggles erupted from me,
Exploring this madness, a true jubilee!

Step into the Uncharted

With socks on the wrong feet, I set off to roam,
Into the uncharted, I felt far from home.
Discovered a cat that wore a top hat,
He said, "Join my Tea Party, just skip the format!"

I tumbled and tripped, it's a wild circus ride,
Where cupcakes are flying and kittens collide.
Put on your best hat, join the zany parade,
For in this odd realm, there's nothing to trade!

Veins of Untold Stories

The coffee shop buzzed, tales swirling in air,
A barista was juggling while brewing with flair.
"Just sip your espresso and watch the show!"
With each quirky story, laughter would flow.

Old pals with new quirks, wild tales in their heads,
From flying cheese wheels to garden gnome dreads.
Each sip brought a chuckle, a fable or two,
Veins of untold stories, both old and brand new!

Awakening the Spirit of Adventure

A squirrel in a hat, so brave and bold,
Dares to climb a tree, stories untold.
With acorns as treasure, he sets his sights,
On a pirate adventure, soaring heights!

With friends by his side, a quirky crew,
A dance-off ensues, oh what a view!
They twirl and they leap, all in good cheer,
An acorn-shaped trophy, a pint of root beer!

Footsteps in Fresh Earth

Worms wiggle and squirm in morning dew,
While frogs wear top hats, quite the debut!
Each footprint a secret, a path not yet made,
As caterpillars giggle at the funny parade.

A rabbit hops by, with juggling skills,
While ants work together, they're king of the hills!
In this muddy ballet, laughter erupts,
As ladybugs cheer, "This way, let's sup!"

Laughter Among the Palms

Underneath the palms, the sun feels just right,
Monkeys play charades under the moonlight.
A toucan yells jokes, and everyone roars,
While a parrot sings tunes, calling out scores!

A picnic of coconuts, what a delight,
With fruit salad games that go on all night.
The rhythm of laughter, a tropical breeze,
As crabs boogie-woogie upon sandy knees!

Shadows of Possibility

The shadows of trees, they dance and they play,
Creating a circus at the end of the day.
An elephant winks with a sly little grin,
As shadows stretch out, let the fun now begin!

A kite soars aloft, it wiggles and spins,
While turtles debate who will win on the fins.
In this whimsical world, there's mischief and calls,
With a sunset finale of shadowy balls!

Beyond the Periphery

In a world of odd and absurd,
Where cats play chess and cows are heard,
I tried to jump on a train of thought,
But missed the platform and tangled, distraught.

With every trip to the shops, I'd find,
New flavors of chips, like pickle pined,
Why not try fish flavored with jam?
Just a snack for this curious ham!

Had a plant that wore sunglasses bright,
Said it needed shade to feel just right,
I told it, "Don't be such a diva,"
It replied, "You need to chill, it's a leaf-iva!"

So here I stand, exploring the quirk,
With puns and giggles, I go to work,
Each step I take leads to silly sights,
In my crazy world where laughter lights.

Navigating New Waters

I bought a kayak for the first time,
Thought I'd glide smoothly, it would be sublime,
But the first paddle made me flip and roll,
Now I'm swimming with fish that tease my soul.

At the beach, seagulls steal my fries,
With beady eyes, they plot and devise,
I swear they hold a secret meeting,
Trying to decide how best to do the cheating!

Once tried to surf on a wave so grand,
Ended up face-first in the soft sand,
While my buddies laughed, I just waved back,
A sunburned face turned self-defense attack!

So I'll stick to floating, no need to race,
With nuggets of joy, I'll find my place,
As I laugh with the tide and water sprite,
Navigating life, what a wacky delight!

Harmonies of Growth

I planted seeds of laughter and cheer,
In a garden where giggles bloom near,
But the carrots dance with a jolly beat,
And brainy broccoli thinks it's elite!

Tomatoes wear shades, feeling so cool,
While strawberries play hopscotch at the school,
As plants recite rhymes to the sky,
I ponder if they ever wonder why?

Each flower struts in a colorful gown,
Competing for buzz from the wandering clown,
I asked the roses how they stay bright,
They winked and said, "Just good vibes and light!"

With every sprout, there's a tale to share,
Of chattering veggies with secrets laid bare,
In this funny patch, I've found my crew,
A garden full of giggles, growing anew!

Unfolding the Map of Life

I bought a map, thought it was grand,
But it showed me donuts in a faraway land,
Chasing cupcakes on this whimsical quest,
I found my heart in sugary zest!

As I wandered off to cookie peaks,
Met a talking llama who shares my leaks,
He said, "To find joy, just follow your nose,"
I laughed so hard, until my sides froze!

Every detour leads to a mishap fun,
Riding with penguins under the sun,
I never knew life could be so absurd,
In a pancake's flip, I found the word!

With each new twist in this map of mine,
I discover delights like a fizzy wine,
So here's to the paths that tickle and tease,
Unfolding adventures that never cease!

The Tangle of Tomorrow

A squirrel named Fred wants to climb high,
He tangled his feet, oh my, oh my!
He thought he was smart, a real tree boss,
But down he went with a comedic toss.

A branch swung low, caught his fuzzy tail,
He spun like a top, a big fluffy sail.
The birds laughed loud, in a twittery cheer,
As Fred learned to dance without any fear.

His lofty dreams turned into a mess,
Leaves in his fur—oh, what a distress!
He aimed for the top, but fell as he played,
Tomorrow's his chance—he won't be dismayed.

Next time, he'll climb with a safer plan,
Wearing a helmet, he's a smart little man.
For when you're up there, keep humor in tow,
Even the fails can give laughs for the show.

Blossoming Ventures

In a garden of giggles, things start to sprout,
A flower named Daisy had doubts, no doubt!
With petals so bright, she jumped in the air,
But landed on Bob, who just didn't care.

Bob was a frog, quite lazy and bored,
He shuffled his feet, and suddenly snored.
Daisy said, "Ribbit! Let's create something neat!"
But Bob just replied with a cute little bleat.

Together they dreamed of a bloom-tastic trend,
A dance for the bugs, they'd invite every friend.
They improvised moves that were silly and sweet,
A joy-filled affair that had everyone beat.

So if you feel stuck, just spring into play,
Flap, flop, or jump, make the most of your day.
For ventures could blossom in sandwiches' shrouds,
With frogs and with flowers, and roars of loud crowds!

The Wishful Wanderer

A mouse named Mia wanted to roam,
From kitchen to garden, she longed for a home.
With dreams of a world made of cheese and delight,
She packed up her snacks, all ready for flight.

She glided past humans, a curious show,
They chased her with brooms, moving fast, oh no!
But Mia just chuckled, she danced through their feet,
A whirlwind of giggles, this mouse is a treat.

She found a tall mushroom, so grand and so round,
Climbed up with finesse, oh what joy she found!
From there she could see all the wonders in sight,
A kingdom of crumbs and the moon's silver light.

So mouse, if you trip or you fall on your quest,
Just laugh it off, dear, and know you're the best.
For wandering wishes can light up the day,
With cheese on the side, you'll find your own way.

A Symphony of Leaves

In a forest so lush, where colors all gleam,
The leaves had a party, a whimsical dream.
They fluttered and giggled, with each little breeze,
Creating a symphony, dancing with ease.

Old Oak played bass, he was tough and so grand,
While Willow swayed softly, a delicate band.
Maple brought colors, a vibrant display,
Each note that they played brought the sun out to play.

But Birch was confused, she just didn't know,
Should she shake to the left or shimmy to flow?
The others all chuckled, "Just follow the beat,
And soon, dear Birch, you'll be hard to beat!"

As twilight descended, they sung and they spun,
With laughter and music, oh what joyous fun!
For leaves in the forest can teach us all, too,
Life's better when dancing with friends, it's true!

The Dance of Divergence

In a forest of choices, we twirl and sway,
Elk in tutus, hippos blushing all day.
They leap and they jump, oh what a sight,
Dancing in circles, well past midnight.

Branches all wiggly, a conga line,
Squirrels holding acorns, sipping on wine.
With each little shimmy, new paths take flight,
Tickling the stumps, oh what pure delight!

A parrot with glasses gives lessons in cheer,
While frogs in bow ties croak loud for a beer.
Each step that we take, there's giggles galore,
Who knew that decision could be such a score?

The more we diverge, the more we connect,
A carnival ride, what's next to expect?
In this dance of life, with laughter galore,
We twirl and we tumble, who could ask for more?

Tides of Change

There's a wave of new snacks on the beach today,
Seagulls are surfing and shouting hooray!
Shells of all flavors, some sweet, some sour,
The ocean, it giggles, like a jester's power.

The sandcastles wobble, the tides drawn near,
With umbrellas as sails and a pint of cold beer.
Crabs are doing yoga, so flexible and spry,
While the starfish are meditating, oh my!

The dolphins are dancing; oh what a sight,
With shades and cocktails, they party all night.
Each dip of the tide brings a laugh and a cheer,
The beach of tomorrow, it's finally here!

Waves crashing low, then up high they rise,
Life's a season of change—a comical surprise!
The ocean keeps speaking in bubbles and foams,
Inviting us all to its water-filled homes.

Kaleidoscope of Growth

A garden of giggles, sprouting each day,
Where carrots wear hats and the lettuce plays.
Tomatoes in shades of pink and green,
They dance when it rains, like a fresh-cut scene.

The daisies all chatter in hues so bright,
While cucumbers slumber, what a silly sight!
Petunias gossip and daisies strut,
In this funny garden, they'll never grow up.

Butterflies hover like quirky old pals,
Spreading their wings, in polka-dot galls.
Bees don't just buzz; they break into song,
Creating a choir where all could belong.

As petals unfurl, new stories unfold,
Jokes sprout from the soil, both cheeky and bold.
In this colorful patch, there's laughter galore,
With a kaleidoscope heart, who could ask for more?

Roots and Wings

With roots deeply planted, the trees do delight,
While birds build their nests in the warm morning light.
Frogs on a trampoline, bouncing with zest,
Roots whisper secrets, a comical quest.

The daisies debate if they should stand tall,
While the hawks above plot a feathered ball.
"Let's fly and let's dance!" the roots cheer with glee,
"Let's grow a wild party and set our souls free!"

The grass does a jig as the wind gives a toss,
While squirrels wear capes pretending to be boss.
In this world of strange wonders, laughter takes wing,
Join roots and the skies for a curious fling!

With every new adventure our laughter takes flight,
From solid foundations, we launch into night.
In this kooky existence of wings and of dirt,
We flourish in chaos, our quirks never hurt.

A Tapestry of Choices

In a world where options dance,
I wear mismatched socks by chance.
Salad for breakfast? Yes, it's a thrill,
But my cat thinks I'm quite the grill.

Should I wear pink or bright green? Oh dear,
My closet's a circus, my fashion unclear.
Flip a coin, let fate take the wheel,
Or just wear pajamas, that's the real deal.

Ice cream for dinner? Don't mind if I do,
Spaghetti with sprinkles, it's all up to you!
Life's a buffet, oh what a delight,
I'll choose dessert first, then the veggies—maybe tonight!

Every decision, a puzzle to solve,
In this wacky world, we happily evolve.
Let's laugh at the choices our lives become,
With a chuckle and grin, let's have some fun!

Silent Conversations with the Sky

I chat with clouds, they're full of sass,
They mock my hair as they gently pass.
They say, 'Get a job, quit dreaming away!'
But I'm busy plotting to steal their sway.

The sun winks at me, grinning wide,
As I try to skateboard down a slide.
'Get ready to tumble!' the wind gives a shout,
But I know I'll just roll, and my friends will pout.

Raindrops giggle, fall like confetti,
Splashing on puddles, always so petty.
I raise my hands, give a great big cheer,
For the sky's sense of humor—it's what brings me near.

Nighttime falls, stars start to chat,
They gossip about where my dog's at.
In this cosmic debate, I sit up high,
Who knew my best friends were up in the sky?

Breakthroughs in the Forest

In the heart of the woods, I came across,
A talking squirrel, the boss of the gloss.
'Got any nuts?' he asked with a grin,
I said, 'Only ideas, let's dive right in!'

He wore a tiny hat, with a feather so proud,
Told me tales of the strangest crowd.
A deer who can tap dance, a bear who sings,
In this comedic woods, joy truly springs.

Branches above, they twist and twirl,
As I stumble around in this leafy whirl.
A raccoon with glasses throws wisdom my way,
'Life's a funny show—enjoy the play!'

I found my way home, a laugh in my heart,
These woodland friends gave my life a fresh start.
Next time I'm lost, I'll just look for the cheer,
And follow the laughter that trails through my sphere.

The Art of New Beginnings

With each sunrise, I wake with a yawn,
Deciding today I'll try something new, maybe dawn.
Trying to bake, but my cookies took flight,
They soared like rockets, oh what a sight!

I painted my walls a vibrant pink,
But ended up drenching the dog—what do you think?
He wears my art like a badge of delight,
With spots and stripes, he's a canvas so bright.

Sock puppets chatter as I sip my tea,
'What's our next venture? Let's climb a tree!'
So I donned my cape, a real hero for sure,
But my hand got stuck—had to call out for more.

Each blunder, a story, each laugh pure gold,
In this dance of missteps, I'm never too old.
So here's to the ventures, both silly and grand,
In the art of new starts, life's a funny band!

Roots and Wings

In a garden full of greens,
A cactus dreamed of becoming beans.
It donned a hat, took to the skies,
Waved at the sun with its prickly thighs.

A daffodil wore silly shoes,
Chasing clouds and making news.
While daisies danced with flapping arms,
And giggled loud at their own charms.

The turnip thought it might go far,
So it painted itself like a rock star.
With wild ambition, it tried to sing,
But only made the bunnies spring.

Roots below were filled with joy,
For every branch is just a ploy.
To lift you up, to make you smile,
And crack a joke every little while.

The Art of Divergence

A tree that wanted to be a fish,
Wiggled its branches, made a wish.
It flopped around in a nearby stream,
Chasing bubbles and ice cream dreams.

The squirrel wore a tiny hat,
And danced around in acrobatic splat.
It tried to leap from branch to branch,
But ended up in the birdies' ranch.

The leaves were tickled by a breeze,
As they sneezed and started to tease.
One shouted, 'Don't be such a bore!
Let's all just twirl a little more!'

And so they tumbled, twirled, and spun,
In a game of hide and seek for fun.
Each time they laughed, they felt so bright,
Creating joy from daylight's light.

Echoes in the Wilderness

In the woods, a tree gave a shout,
Echoes bounced, what was that about?
A raccoon replied with a cheeky grin,
'You're just jealous of my vintage tin!'

The owls rolled their eyes, so wise,
As they muttered under moonlit skies.
'Who needs a crown when you've got flair?
We'll host a party, if you dare!'

A wildflower came with a dance,
Twirling bees in a merry trance.
They bumbled in, a buzzing crew,
To join the fun, as friendships grew.

Echoes rang through the fun-filled night,
As trees and critters danced with delight.
In the wilderness, all hearts would sing,
Of silly things that laughter bring.

Divergent Trails

Down by the river where the critters roam,
A turtle decided to leave home.
With a knapsack full of snacks to munch,
It waddled off to join the lunch crunch.

A rabbit fast and dressed quite fine,
Thought it could take a longer line.
But found itself at the wrong buffet,
Where sloths served up the meal of the day.

The path was filled with chuckles loud,
As every critter formed a crowd.
Each telling tales of their wild quest,
Finding adventure in every jest.

By the end of the day, they grew quite wise,
Realizing fun was the biggest prize.
So whatever trail you decide to choose,
Remember, laughter is the best muse.

Unraveling Paths

In the garden, I took a turn,
Found a weed that just won't burn.
It winked at me, said with a grin,
"I'm the champion of 'don't let me in!"

Through the maze of green, I tripped and laughed,
Found a path that was truly daft.
A gnome waved by with a cheeky cheer,
Spinning tales of where to steer!

Each step forward felt quite absurd,
Like chasing chirps from a flying bird.
With twists and turns that made me zany,
Each corner turned feels more than crazy!

Still I wander, can't find my way,
Armed with snacks to fuel the fray.
Life's a puzzle with no clear plan,
I'll just dance, and play, and spin like a fan!

Nature's Divergence

In the woods, the trees have secrets,
Some wear hats, some have regrets.
A squirrel chattered, "Pick a lane!"
"Choose a route, or go insane!"

I thought I'd follow the buzzing bees,
They led me straight to a swarm of fleas.
"Not this way!" I called out loud,
As I stumbled through the tiny crowd.

A rabbit hopped by, sporting shades,
"Try this trail, it never fades!"
But all it led to was a muddy patch,
Where my shoes got stuck, quite a catch!

So, I laugh and turn around,
Finding joy where lost is found.
Nature's ways are a quirky dance,
And life's a joke, just take a chance!

Infinite Vines

Vines everywhere, they stretch and creep,
Like my dreams after a late night's sleep.
I tried to climb, but tripped on my shoes,
Now I'm tangled; it's no excuse!

"Help!" I yelled to a passing snail,
It shrugged and said, "I'm slow, but not frail!"
We discussed the merits of taking it slow,
As the vines nearby took over the show.

Twisting and curling, they upward climb,
Making patterns that mess with time.
"It's a workout!" I said with a grin,
Though my legs are sore from this vine-y spin!

Laughter echoes through the leafy maze,
I've found new friends in the strangest ways.
So here I stand, a vine-draped champ,
Living life like a whimsical lamp!

The Journey of Growth

Once a seed, now a sprouting mess,
Dreaming big, though I must confess.
I stretched my roots, hitched a ride,
With a worm who said, "Let's take a slide!"

Upward I climbed, with leaves unfurled,
Caught in the wind, I spun and twirled.
"Watch your balance!" shouted a frog,
As I wobbled high on a downy log.

Sunshine and rain made me yippee,
"Don't forget to water me!" said the bee.
We giggled and chuckled, friends in bloom,
While dancing to nature's silly tune.

Growth is chaos, a merry jest,
Like a jigsaw puzzle, but not quite the best.
Yet in the mess and the laughs we find,
A joy in living, forever entwined!

New Horizons

I once was a twig, barely a sprout,
Dreaming of places, outside my route.
A gust came along, I wiggled with glee,
Now I'm a tree, oh, look at me!

The winds started swirling, I danced like a fool,
Poking my leaves in the neighbor's pool.
A bee landed near, whispered sweet things,
With dreams of exploring, and other fun flings.

I rolled with the laughter, so carefree and spry,
Chasing the clouds, oh, me oh my!
The squirrels told tales of wild escapades,
While I, toothy grin, let my laughter cascade.

So here's to the branches, both big and small,
Life's a wild ride when you're having a ball.
With roots in the ground, and sky up above,
Funny how far we can stretch with some love!

Beyond the Roots

Beneath the ground, my roots dug so deep,
While I tell the earth, 'Don't worry, I'll creep!'
A gopher came by, said, "You look quite round,"
I huffed and I puffed, and I'd never back down.

I thought of my branches, so high up in space,
Tickling the clouds, in a crazy race.
My leaves began rustling, gossiping dear,
Of hilarious tales they overheard all year.

Then came a woodpecker, pecking away,
"Hey tree, why so serious? Let's dance and play!"
We wiggled and jiggled, what a sight indeed,
Who knew that a trunk could be such a steed?

So here's to the roots, that keep me secure,
And to all those adventures, oh what a lure!
I'll reach for the stars and swing high with glee,
For the laughter of life is the best cup of tea.

Treetop Dreams

Up high in my branches, I peer at the land,
With a grin so wide, my dreams feel quite grand.
A squirrel named Doug brought his acorn stash,
He said, 'Let's aim for that house with the flash!'

I thought of my twigs, so sturdy and bold,
Eager for laughter, and stories retold.
With leaves shouting cheer, we planned quite a feast,
For a party on branches, where dreams get released.

The critters all gathered, oh what a sight,
Dancing and prancing, we laughed through the night.
A raccoon brought cookies, a spread so divine,
And a frog served up punch, with a big glass of shine.

So here in the treetops, I hope you will see,
The fun that we have, the wild jubilee!
Life's full of laughter when you sway with the breeze,
And dance with your friends among the tall trees.

Expanding Canopy

I started as a seed, snug in my shell,
But a grand adventure was ringing a bell.
A robin flew by, said, "Come on, take flight!"
So I grew my branches with all of my might.

The sun brought a chuckle, with rays that were bright,
As I stretched my green arms, oh what a sight!
The ants held a meeting, in circles they spun,
Organizing a dance, and oh, it was fun!

I offered my shade to the critters below,
With laughter and joy, what a wonderful show!
They gathered in droves, a party so loud,
A canopy grand, with joy that would crowd.

So here's to the growing, let's reach for the sky,
With friends by your side, just let your heart fly.
In whispers of leaves, adventures are near,
Let's giggle and frolic, with nothing to fear!

Lateral Whispers

In the garden of thoughts, ideas sprout,
With a wink and a nod, they twist about.
One says, 'I'm a tree, watch me grow!'
The other replies, 'But I'm more of a bush, you know!'

Under the sun, they giggle and sway,
Speaking in whispers, come join the play.
Leaves tickle the sky, roots tangle below,
While the squirrels debate who will steal the show.

A rose claims it's bold, while violets shy away,
Thorns throw a tantrum, 'Why must we stay?'
Daisies dance in circles, thinking they're stars,
And the cacti joke, 'We've got the best bars!'

In this garden of jest, there's laughter galore,
Each petal a pun, each bud wanting more.
So if you're feeling stuck or a little down,
Just listen to nature, it's the silliest crown.

Offshoots of Destiny

Amid the wild woods, strange paths do appear,
A pine told a tale that no one could hear.
'I'll start a new trend, just you wait and see!'
While a maple spouted, 'I'll be twirlier than me!'

The birch gave a laugh, 'Oh, look at us all!'
As they plotted a course for a nature-wide ball.
The ferns wiggled to one side, feeling quite grand,
While acorns prepared for a royal bandstand.

Mushrooms were munching, pretending to be cool,
While the willows formed lines for a dance at the school.
"A twist and a shout!" each sapling did cheer,
As leaves tossed their hats, 'This is our year!'

With laughter like echoes, the branches all bowed,
In this leafy affair, they danced strong and proud.
For fun, they declared, they could leap and they'd sway,
As the sun painted pictures, fading worry away!

Ventures into the Unknown

Away from the trunk, where the wild things play,
Little shoots gleefully giggle and sway.
'Let's wander this way, oh what could we find?'
While the older trees groaned, 'You're out of your mind!'

They climbed over stones, jumped onto logs,
Dodged a few skunks and series of frogs.
With each little giggle, they sparked a surprise,
While the weeds rolled their eyes at the daring reprise.

"What's that in the shadows?" one sprout whispered low,
"It's just wizard mushrooms with a jaunty bow!"
They tiptoed in circles, gave a green howl,
As the wind chuckled softly, 'Oh, such a prowl!'

By the end of the day, they returned with a grin,
With tales of adventure, how could they not win?
Though older trees tutted, 'Oh what a show!'
The young ones just smiled, ready for more!

Leafy Explorations

In the realm of green, with laughter afloat,
A bold little sprout claimed, 'I'll be a boat!'
'The currents of branches, in skies oh so blue,'
While the daisies just giggled, 'We'll join you too!'

They set sail on pollen, riding high on the breeze,
Singing sweet songs like honey from bees.
A sunflower shouted, 'Look, I can fly!'
As they drifted through dreams, with the clouds oh so shy.

But a breeze came along, and oh did they twirl,
Spinning and flipping, each leaf in a whirl.
While the roots on the ground just watched in dismay,
A chorus of chuckles in nature's cabaret.

They landed in laughter, all tangled and spun,
With stories of mischief, oh weren't they just fun?
Under the sun's glow, they shared their grand tales,
Of leafy adventures and whimsy-filled trails!

Scattered Possessions

My socks play hide and seek, they roll,
In laundry piles, they lose control.
One's here, the other's far away,
They plot together for a game to play.

My keys are on a secret quest,
They take a trip, I need a rest.
They lead me out, then go and hide,
In couch cushions, they won't abide.

My glasses sit, a cheeky pair,
On top my head, without a care.
When I do find them, I squint and huff,
They laugh aloud, 'You found us, tough!'

The remote just vanished, how bizarre,
It's hiding under the cookie jar.
I shake my head at this silly ruse,
In my home, the objects just refuse!

Vistas of the Mind

Thoughts drift like balloons in a breeze,
They float and twist, doing as they please.
One pops with laughter, another just sighs,
As unicorns argue 'neath cotton-candy skies.

A dragonfly scribbles a grocery list,
While talking hedgehogs insist to assist.
But maybe they'll nibble on all the bread,
And I'll end up with a grumpy head.

Ideas bust out like confetti at noon,
They tumble and dance, like a wacky cartoon.
A giraffe wearing glasses critiques my plans,
With giggles and snorts, it waves its hands.

So here's to the chaos that spins in my brain,
A circus of creatures, both silly and sane.
As I sip my coffee, a thought frolics free,
And who knows what's next? Maybe tea with a bee!

Stirrings of the Soul

My soul woke up with a loud 'surprise!'
It chucked its blanket, and rubbed its eyes.
With a hop and a skip, it raced for the door,
Yelling, 'Life's an adventure, come see what's in store!'

It tripped on a cloud, took a tumble, then spun,
Said, 'Life is better when you're having fun!'
A nest of giggles and songs filled the air,
As it danced with shadows, without a care.

It tickled a dream that lay on the ground,
And made it laugh with a silly sound.
Then off it darted, through laughter and light,
Dragging my heart to a joyous height.

So if you see my soul out on the street,
Tell it I miss its whimsical beat.
Chasing after smiles like a puppy so bold,
In a world full of wonder, we enjoy the gold.

Shadows of Inquiry

Questions wiggle like worms in the dirt,
Tickling minds, and making them squirt.
Why does the toaster burn only my bread?
And why is my cat always plotting instead?

I ponder about socks, where do they roam?
Are they living it up in some far-off home?
With parties and friends that make them feel whole,
While I'm left here, just missing my coal.

Why do we laugh when we feel quite blue?
Is it nature's way of making us new?
Perhaps I'll ask a wise cactus near,
With a jabbering squirrel, who's loud and clear.

In shadows of inquiry, we dance with the strange,
With chuckles and nudges, we seek to exchange.
So let's keep asking, let curiosity reign,
For questions are flowers in life's wild terrain.

Whispers of New Frontiers

In the garden of dreams, I found a sprout,
It said, "Hey there, buddy, let's go check it out!"
With my slippers on and my hair all a mess,
We ventured to places that I couldn't guess.

The daisies were dancing, the sun wore a grin,
I asked a big mushroom, "Where do we begin?"
He chuckled and replied, "Just follow your nose,
Adventure awaits where the wild clover grows!"

We jumped over puddles that giggled with glee,
The ants held a party, just you wait and see!
With a picnic of pickles and jelly on bread,
We toasted to journeys and none were misled.

So next time you wander, don't stay on the ground,
Listen to whispers that tell tales profound.
With laughter and joy, life's a delightful spree,
Join the merry mischief, come dance with me!

A Journey in the Leaves

Once I grabbed a snack and a crunchy old leaf,
It whispered to me, "Hey, let's be a chief!"
I donned my crown made of twigs and some glue,
We marched on a quest, just me and my stew.

The squirrels were chuckling, the winds made a sound,
As we traveled through places where silliness found.
I tried to be serious, but tripped on a root,
The leaves laughed so hard, oh my, what a hoot!

We found a tall tree with a sign that said "Climb,"
I just shook my head, "I'm not in my prime!"
But up with a grumble, I went to the sky,
And traded my worries for butterflies high.

So grab a good leaf, let your silliness flow,
Adventure is waiting, let giggles bestow.
Life's such a ride when you don't take a fall,
On this grand journey, let laughter be all!

Tides of Aspiration

The ocean called loudly with waves full of cheer,
I built me a castle, my crown made of beer.
With a bucket for dreams, I scooped out some fun,
And danced with the dolphins as the day was done.

The seagulls all squawked, they joined in the game,
With fish in their beaks, they all laughed at my name.
"Oh captain of folly, please sail us away!"
We surfed on the tides, what a wonderful day!

Just then a big wave gave everyone fright,
I slipped on a crab and took flight like a kite.
But laughter erupted from all who had seen,
As I landed in sand that was yellow and green.

So when life brings you waves, just grab on and ride,
With friends by your side, let your heart be your guide.
These tides of ambition can stumble you flat,
But with giggles and smiles, no worries to chat!

The Echo of Longing

In a field of desires, a bell started to ring,
I chased after the sound, what joy it could bring!
The rabbits looked on with their ears all perked,
As I tripped over daisies, a bit mad and lurked.

The echo continued, it bounced off some trees,
It said, "Hey there, buddy, just do as you please!"
I hollered right back, "Where are you, my friend?"
Through giggles and chuckles, we'd laugh till the end.

I found a fat frog who croaked with delight,
"Follow my sound, I'll lead you tonight!"
We leapt through the meadow, my heart full of spree,
With echoes of laughter from all that I'd see.

So if you feel lost, just listen and leap,
The echoes of joy will never go cheap.
Adventure awaits if you're willing to sing,
In a world full of wonders, just see what it brings!

Ephemeral Journeys

We set off with a map untraced,
With snacks more than we could have faced.
Our compass spun like a disco ball,
We laughed till we couldn't recall.

Each twist and turn was quite absurd,
We misread signs; oh, how we blurred!
Found a field that claimed it was rare,
Turned out to be just a cow's chair.

In search of treasures lost in dreams,
We stumbled, fell, and lost our schemes.
A tree with branches waving high,
Gave us the giggles, oh me, oh my!

At riverside, with fish and fries,
We swore we'd seen a turtle fly.
But that was just our lunch's flair,
As we chewed with the utmost care.

Echoes of Exploration

Into the woods we bravely strode,
With wiggly sticks and bags we towed.
An echo called, we thought it was fun,
'Til we learned it was a scared raccoon run!

Through thickets thick, we heard a shout,
Was it a bear? Nope, just our clout.
We tripped and tumbled, what a scene,
As tree roots played a cruel routine.

A sign that read: 'Lost? Take a peek!'
We couldn't laugh; it was getting bleak.
But in the end, we made a friend,
A squirrel named Nutty— our hero, no end!

The journey's wild, the laughs are clear,
With Nutty here, we've got no fear.
As dusk approached, snacks came in,
With cookies crumbled, let the giggles begin!

Sunlit Adventures

Under the sun, our quest began,
With shades and drinks, a silliness plan.
We chased the wind, on bicycles old,
Hollering stories of treasures untold.

A rainbow path made of ice cream cones,
We sang with joy, ignoring our phones.
With every pedal, we painted the day,
Till ice cream dripped in a colorful spray!

Uphill we climbed, but oh that hill,
Each pedal forward gave quite the thrill.
A bird swooped down and stole our fries,
We laughed so hard, we nearly cried.

As sunset approached with golden rays,
We spun in circles, lost in a daze.
With a final giggle, we rode down fast,
In sunlit moments, forever to last.

Threads of Transformation

With yarn in hand, we sat to create,
Knots and loops that twisted their fate.
Our garments grew with every cheer,
'Till we wore sweaters that brought on jeers!

A scarf that flopped; it touched the floor,
A hat that perched like a laundry chore.
Each stitch we made, a laugh ensued,
Who knew crafting could change our mood?

A friendship formed through fabric's wiles,
Spinning tales, sharing styles.
We made a quilt with patches bright,
With all our dreams stitched up tight!

As colors clashed, we danced about,
In threads of laughter, we spun our shout.
In every mishap, we found delight,
Transforming chaos into pure light.

The Map of Potential

A treasure map drawn in crayon,
With dotted lines and a big red X,
Follow the path where squirrels run,
Avoiding the sneaky raccoon complex.

There's a path through the bakery,
Where pastries dance and pies can sing,
But watch out for the flour tornado,
That'll give your nose a sneeze-bling.

The juice stand is a hotspot,
With flavors that twist and twirl,
Order a 'berry-banana-bomb',
And watch those taste buds swirl!

Keep your eyes peeled for magic trees,
That sprinkle wishes with every breeze,
Just don't get caught in the gumdrop mud,
Or you'll be stuck in a sticky squeeze.

Twists and Turns of Fate

Life's a rollercoaster ride,
With loops and spins too wild to bear,
Strap in tight, hold on to your snack,
Or risk a flying cheesy affair.

A cactus on the track ahead,
Looks oddly like a green balloon,
You might just dodge or take a poke,
Either way, you'll laugh at noon.

Take a fork, dive left or right,
As ducks all quack a funny beat,
Hilarious mishaps, a laughing spree,
As fate plays hide and seek on repeat.

What a lively journey this all be,
With every twist, oh can't you see?
A merry dance through hiccups and blunders,
Fate's just a jolly joker, that's glee.

Unfurling Dreams

In the garden where ideas bloom,
There's a gnome who tap-dances at night,
With a top hat made of macaroni,
And dreams that tackle every fright.

Bouncing thoughts like a pogo stick,
They spring up wild, they leap around,
Just watch out for the dreaming cat,
She'll snooze and turn your hopes upside down.

Join the parade of drifting schemes,
Where unicorns hold hula-hoops tight,
Every wish a swirling delight,
Let's twirl and giggle till morning light.

Each laughter stirs the petals wide,
As daydreams take a slide,
In this reckless hop into the skies,
Nothing's too silly, in our minds, we ride.

Beyond the Comfort Zone

Got your suitcase packed with snacks?
Ready to leap from cozy and sweet,
The couch greets you with a sad sigh,
While new adventures tap their feet.

Flip-flops on a winter's day,
Walk that line of fashion loot,
With ice-cream cones in your mittens,
Life's a laugh, and who's to dispute?

There's a bouncy castle at the end,
Where grown-ups bounce like silly kids,
Laughing at rules that once held tight,
Now tossed away like old pudding lids.

Unzip your heart and let it play,
Go beyond where comfort strays,
For life's a stage designed for fun,
Step off the edge and aim for sun.

www.ingramcontent.com/pod-product-compliance
Lightning Source LLC
Chambersburg PA
CBHW070750220426
43209CB00083B/359